W9-CHS-588

·I love you·

by
Lauren White

**Andrews McMeel
Publishing**
Kansas City

♡ LOVE NAMES ♡

sweetie

light of
my life

bunny

pumpkin

honey pie

petal

princess

sweetheart

baby

sole mate!

flower

dreamboat

angel

sugar

pudding

sunshine

kitten

honey

rosebud

ball and chain!

little peach

"love me...

...love my sense of humor"

will you be my valentine ?

adam

eve

FOOD FOR LOVERS

champagne

strawberries

oysters

honey

dates

nasturtium

caviar

cream

mango

chocolates

asparagus

truffles

figs

cinnamon

ice cream

jasmine tea

peeled grapes

turkish delight

mussels

"love me...

...love my dog"

♡ · KISSING WITH CONFIDENCE · ♡

(i) Clean teeth until they sparkle
   (No fragments of spinach or garlic breath)

(ii) Relax and move closer

(iii) Close eyes and pucker up

(iv) Enjoy!

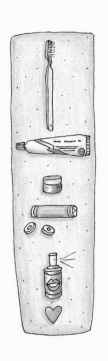

josephine

loves me not • loves me • loves me not • loves me • loves me • loves me not • loves me. loves me not. loves me. loves me not. loves me. loves me not. loves me. loves

"love me...

... love my work"

·a romantic evening·

red rose   candlelight   red wine

moonlit sky

tom

jerry

sometimes you're a...

prickly cactus

cold fish

sack of potatoes

"love me...

... love my friends"

sometimes you're a ...

cuddly teddy bear

sex bomb!

ray of sunshine

Samson

delilah

when you're in love...

the world turns upside down

"love me...

love my little fibs!"

· breakfast in bed ·

basket of bagels

flowers   coffee   lots of pillows

antony

cleopatra

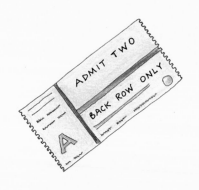

"of all the gin-joints
in all the world...
you had to walk
into mine"

"love me...

...love my habits"

THE LANGUAGE OF FLOWERS

lily·of·the·valley~
happiness

poppy~
consolation

carnation~
sadness in love

yellow rose~
jealousy

white rose~
worthiness

red rose~
true love

red tulip~
declaration
of love

jasmine ~
amiability

sweet pea ~
departure

marigold ~
grief.

forget-me-not ~
forget me not!

love·in·a·mist ~
perplexity

clematis ~
beautiful thoughts

daisy ~
innocence

bay ~
glory

bacall

LOVE SICKNESS

loss of appetite

daydreaming

racing heart

lack of concentration

childish behavior

mood swings

"love me...

... love my singing '

together we can ⌒

sail across the clouds...

catch moonbeams...

slide down a rainbow...

· moonbeam ·

rhett

scarlett

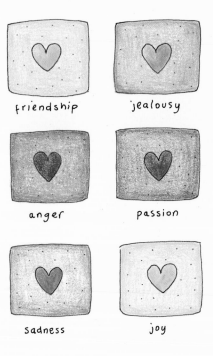

THE COLORS OF LOVE

friendship jealousy

anger passion

sadness joy

"love me...

... love my hairstyle"

I
want
to
share
everything
with
you
♡

jerry

I wear my heart on my:

sleeve

pocket

lapel

trouser leg

shoe

hat

"love me...

... *love my mess* "

I want the world to know how much I love you...

GREAT PARTNERSHIPS Nº9

robin hood

maid marian

heart-shaped things

petal

strawberry

leaf

chili pepper

"love me...

...love my driving"

I wish I could make myself tiny and hide in your pocket...

strawberries

cream

· a little message ·

"love me...

...love my daydreaming"

fred.

.ginger.

I'd like us to grow old together...

"love me...

...love my impatience"

∂·LOVE POTIONS·ß

rosemary

pansy juice

honeysuckle

sprig of
thyme

lettuce

quince

laurel twigs

wild arum

herb paris

ash leaves

cyclamen

cinnamon

vervain

romeo

juliet

we fit!

"love me...

... love my dancing"

you're just right !

·me·

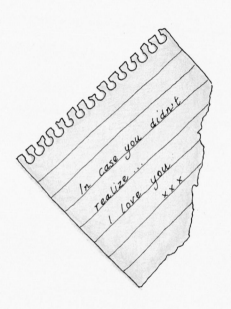

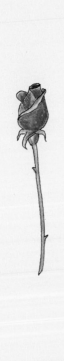

"Adding a sprinkling of magic to the everyday..." is how Lauren White describes her original style of drawing. Born and brought up in the village of Cranfield in Bedfordshire County, England, she studied fine art in Hull and London before returning to Bedfordshire to work as resident illustrator for a local wildlife trust. Lauren loves playing the piano, walking her dog Jack, and she carries a sketchbook everywhere she goes. She lives with her partner, Michael, and describes herself as having an astonishing collection of marbles and a wicked sense of humor. Lauren's designs for Hotchpotch greetings cards are sold around the world, and in this book she continues to refine her distinctive style which "celebrates the simple things in life."

First published by MQ Publications Limited
254–258 Goswell Road, London EC1V 7RL

Copyright © MQ Publications Limited 1999
Text & Illustrations © Lauren White 1999

ISBN: 0-8362-9649-4

Library of Congress Catalog Card Number: 98-88409

99 00 01 02 03 MQP 10 9 8 7 6 5 4 3 2 1

www.andrewsmcmeel.com

Printed and bound in Malaysia